CEREBRAL WAR

©By Michael K. Mattox, Sr. 11-13-2014; Thursday 6:07p.m. 36 sec. (Non-Fiction)

Table of Contents

57	58	59	60	61	62	63	64
49	50	51	52	53	54	55	56
41	42	43	44	45	46	47	48
33	34	35	36	37	38	39	40
25	26	27	28	29	30	31	30

17	18	19	20	21	22	23	24
9	10	11	12	13	14	15	16
1	2	3	4	5	6	7	8

i

Vertical Line

ii

Horizontal line

iii

Diagonal line right

iv

Diagonal line left

v

Black King on its black color square

vi

White King on the opposite colored square

My Thesis Statement: What is ***Cerebral War? Cerebral War*** is the "Battle of the Minds" or "Competition of the Minds," "Mind vs. Mind," "My Mind vs. Your Mind" in an intellectual competition. To out-think or outmaneuver your opponent mentally or intellectually; using your cognitive faculty thinking skills.

To be successful in ***"Cerebral War"*** it is mandatory must that you have ***Game!***

What is ***Game?*** The definition of ***Game*** has 6 different components.

Game is:

1) Wisdom;
2) Knowledge;
3) Understanding;
4) Most Aggressive Strategy;
5) Taking Massive Actions; and
6) Do It Now.

<u>Assassinatas' Chess Club Rules:</u>

1) Play your opponent in chess in your head w/o the board and chess pieces in front of you; with the new & best ***Chess Numeric Notation System.***
2) Assassinatas' position pieces the same as the traditional chess system except; the King is on its color square, not the Queen on her color square as the traditional chess system. (*See diagrams on page vi and vii*).
3) Another difference is that the ***Black Chess*** go first not the white chess pieces as it is with the traditional chess system.
4) Black chess pieces are on the highest number squares and white chess pieces are on the lowest number squares, and;
5) If pawn makes it to the 8th rank it can promote to any chess piece including the king and/or not promote remaining a pawn; but the pawn can only promote to king if it will not be in check; forcing the opponent to have to check mate both kings; if this is impossible then it is a draw!

2

Glossary:

Vertical= directly up and/or down

Horizontal= left and/or right across

Diagonal=slanted up or down

Columns=are all squares going in the up and down position, vertical

Ranks/Rows= are all squares going across, horizontal

3

**Breaking down the chess system and formulas:**

The chess board is divided into 64 squares;8 by 8;8 squares right to left (horizontally) are called ranks/rows. There are 8 total ranks. 8 squares up and down (vertically) are called columns; there are 8 total columns.

As you see, on the diagram on page (i), at the bottom left dark colored corner is square #1. The first 8 horizontal row of squares are numbered individually in their own squares; #1 thru #8 in sequential order starting at the left dark square going to the right squares. Each square has its own individual square number. The second horizontal row of squares are numbered #9 thru #16 following the same pattern stated above and follows the same sequential order for the rest of the rows for numbering the squares; starting at the closes left square going to the farthest right square. The third row is numbered #17 thru #24; the fourth row/rank is numbered #25 thru #32; the fifth row is numbered #33 thru #40; the sixth row is numbered #41 thru #48; the seventh row is numbered #49 thru #56; and the eighth row is numbered #57 thru #64.

With the lower numbers facing you the 4 corner square numbers should be #1 at the lower left dark colored corner square; #8 at the lower right light colored corner square; #57 at the upper left light colored corner square; and #64 at the upper right dark colored corner square.

4

Formulas for when the lowest square numbers are facing you:

Formula #1: starting on square #1; if you want to move a chess piece 1 square horizontally to the right add 1 (+1). That would put you on square #2. Starting at square #2, if you want to move a chess piece 1 square horizontally to the left subtract 1 (-1). *Notice you cannot go 1 square horizontally left from square #1. Also notice you cannot go 1 square horizontally right from square #8; you will arrive on the second row landing on square #9. (+1) from square #16 you will arrive on the third row landing on square #17;(+1) from square #24 you will arrive on the fourth row landing on square #25;(+1) from square #32 you will arrive on the fifth row landing on square #33;(+1) from square #40 you will arrive on the sixth row landing on squares #41;(+1) from square #48 you will arrive at the seventh row landing on square #49;(+1) from square #56 you will arrive on the eighth row landing on square #57.

Ranks/rows are horizontal left to right. To move a chess piece to the direct right square, take the square number & (+1).

To move a chess piece to the direct left square, take the square number & (-1).

Ranks #1, squares left to right are numbered:

1,2,3,4,5,6,7,8;

Ranks #2, squares left to right are numbered:
9,10,11,12,13,14,15,16;

5

Ranks #3, squares left to right are
numbered:17,18,19,20,21,22,23,24;

Ranks #4, squares left to right are numbered:
25,26,27,28,292,30,31,32;

Ranks #5, squares left to right are numbered:
33,34,35,36,37,38,39,40

Ranks #6, squares left to right are numbered:
41,42,43,44,45,46,47,48;

Ranks #7, squares left to right are numbered:
49,50,51,52,53,54,55,56;

Ranks #8, squares left to right are numbered:
57,58,59,60,61,62,63,64.

Formula #2: to move a chess piece one square up vertically, take the square number & add 8 (+8) to get to the square in that same column directly up (vertical) from that square number you stared at. To get to the previous square number in that same vertical column, take the square number & subtract 8 (-8).

   *Remember, columns are vertical up and down.

Column #1, squares starting down going up are numbered: 1,9,17,25,33,41,49,57;

Column #2, squares starting down going up are numbered: 2,10,18,26,34,42,50,58;

Column #3, squares starting down going up are numbered: 3,11,19,27,35,43,51,59;

6

Column #4, squares starting down going up are numbered: 4,12,20,28,36,44,52,60;

Column #5, squares starting down going up are numbered: 5,13,21,29,37,45,53,61

Column #6, squares starting down going up are numbered: 6,14,22,30,38,46,54,62;

Column #7, squares starting down going up are numbered: 7,15,23,31,39,47,55,63;

Column #8, squares starting down going up are numbered: 8,16,24,32,40,48,56,64.

   Formula #3: to move a chess piece to the upper right diagonal adjacent square take the square number and add 9 (+9). To move a chess piece back to the lower left diagonal square take the square number and subtract 9 (-9). Remember diagonal squares are the slanted adjacent squares going up or down.

Diagonal square numbers going to the upper right diagonal adjacent squares starting on square #2 are: 2,11,20,29,38,47,56;

Diagonal square numbers going to the upper right diagonal adjacent squares starting on square #3 are: 3,12,21,30,39,48; Diagonal square numbers going to the upper right diagonal adjacent squares starting on square #4 are: 4,13,22,31,40; Diagonal square numbers going to the upper right diagonal adjacent squares starting on square #5 are: 5,14,23,32;

Diagonal square numbers going to the upper right diagonal

7

adjacent squares starting on square #6 are: 6,15,24;

Diagonal square numbers going to the upper right diagonal adjacent squares starting on square #7 are: 7,16

Diagonal square numbers going to the upper right diagonal adjacent squares starting on square #9 are: 9,18,27,36,45,54,63;

   *(+9) starting on square #10 the upper right diagonal adjacent squares are the same formula (formula #3) for starting on square #1 except, you start with that particular, same for starting on square numbers: 19,28,37,46,55,64.

Diagonal square numbers going to the upper right diagonal adjacent squares starting on square #17 are: 17,26,35,44,53,62.

*(+9) starting on square #18 the upper right diagonal adjacent squares are the same formula, (formula #3) for starting on square #9 except, you start with that particular square, same for starting on square numbers: 27,36,45,54,63.

Diagonal square numbers going to the upper right diagonal adjacent squares starting on square #25 are: 25,34,43,52,61; Diagonal square numbers going to the upper right diagonal adjacent squares starting on square #33 are: 33,42,51,60.

*(+9) starting on square #34 the upper right diagonal adjacent squares are the same formula, (formula #3) for starting on square #25 except, you start with that particular square, same for starting on square numbers: 43,52,61.

Diagonal square numbers going to the upper right diagonal

8

adjacent squares starting on square #41 are: 41,50,59.

*(+9) starting on square #42 the upper right diagonal adjacent squares are the same formula, (formula #3) for starting on square #33 except, you start with that particular square, same for starting on square numbers: 51,60.

*(+9) starting on square #50 the upper right diagonal adjacent squares are the same formula, (formula #3) for starting on square #41 except, you start with that particular square, same for starting on square number is #59.

*Square numbers: 8,16,24,32,40,48,56,57,58,60,61,62,63,64 do not have the upper right diagonal adjacent squares. Why? Because those squares are on the edge of the board.

Formula #4: if you want a chess piece to move to the upper left diagonal adjacent square, take that square number and add 7 (+7). To move the chess piece back to the lower right diagonal adjacent square take the square number and subtract 7 (-7).

Diagonal square numbers going to the upper left diagonal adjacent squares starting on square #2 gets you to square #9.

Diagonal square numbers going to the upper left diagonal adjacent squares starting on square #3 are: 3,10,17;

Diagonal square numbers going to the upper left diagonal adjacent squares starting on square #4 are: 4,11,18,25;

Diagonal square numbers going to the upper left diagonal adjacent squares starting on square #5 are: 5,12,19,26,33;

Diagonal square numbers going to the upper left diagonal adjacent squares starting on square #6 are: 6,13,20,27,34,41;
Diagonal square numbers going to the upper left diagonal adjacent squares starting on square #7 are: 7,14,21,28,35,42,49;

Diagonal square numbers going to the upper left diagonal adjacent squares starting on square #8 are: 8,15,22,36,43,50,57.

*(+7) starting on square #10 the upper left diagonal adjacent squares are the same formula (formula #4) for starting on square #2 except, you start with that particular, same for starting on square numbers: 11,12,13,14,15,16.

Diagonal square numbers going to the upper left diagonal adjacent squares starting on square #24 are: 24,31,38,45,52,59; Diagonal square numbers going to the upper left diagonal adjacent squares starting on square #32 are: 32,39,46,53,60; Diagonal square numbers going to the upper left diagonal adjacent squares starting on square #40 are: 40,47,54,61; Diagonal square numbers going to the upper left diagonal adjacent squares starting on square #48 are: 48,55,62;

Diagonal square numbers going to the upper left diagonal adjacent squares starting on square #56 is 63.

   *You cannot go to the upper left diagonal adjacent squares starting on square numbers:
1,9,17,25,33,41,49,57,58,59,60,61,62,63,64.

Why? Because those squares are on the edge of the board & do

10

not have an upper left diagonal adjacent square.

   Summary, moving rank to rank; when you are playing the white chess pieces the low square numbers are facing you. The formula is (+9), (+8), (+7) from that particular square number; in which; determines the destination of that distinctive chess pieces' particular move at that given point in time.

Formula #5: moving rank to rank; when the higher square numbers of the board are facing you, which is the position of the black chess pieces; the formula is (-9), (-8), (-7) from that particular square number; which determines your destination of that distinctive chess pieces' particular move at that given point in time.

*Remember, when playing black chess pieces; the formula to move up a square from that rank to the next rank is to take the square number and subtract 8 (-8). Example, square #64 to square #56 is 64-8=square #56. This is where your chess piece will arrive. *That's moving up opposite from when the lowest square numbers are facing you; when you are playing white chess pieces; starting at square numbers 1 thru 8. To move back rank to rank when highest numbers are facing you (playing black chess pieces) you would go square 56 – 8= square #64.

11

To get to the upper right diagonal squares for bishops, Queens, and Kings you would (-9). Starting on square #63 to get to the upper right diagonal square, you would go square #63-9=square #54. To get back to square #63 from square #54, which is the lower left diagonal square, you would go square

#54+9=square #63. *Remember your playing black chess pieces so the highest numbers are always facing you the chess player.

When you're the black chess pieces the highest numbers are facing you. To get to the upper left diagonal squares (-7). Starting on square #63; you would go square #63-7=square #56. To get back to square #63 the lower right diagonal square (+7); you would go square #56+7=square #63.

To go up a square puts you on the upper rank (-8). Starting on square #63, you would go square #63-8=square #55. To go back to square #63 from square #55, you would go square #55+8=square #63

When the lowest numbers are facing you which is square #1; to get to the next rank square #9. You would go square # 1+8=square #9 which moves forward. To move backwards from square #9 to square #1; you would go square #9-8=square #1.

To move to square #2 from square #1, you would go square #1+1=square #2; to move back to square #1 from square #2, you would go square #2-1=square #1.

Starting on square #10 going diagonally up to the upper right square #19, you would go square #10+9=square #19. To move

12

back to square #10 from square #19, you would go square #19-9=square #10(lower left diagonal square).

Starting on square #15 to get to square #22 which is the upper left diagonal square, you would go square #15+7=square

#22. To go back to square #15 from square #22, you would go square #22-7=square #15, which is the lower right diagonal square.

Starting at square #3 to go to square #11, you would go square#3+8=square #11. To go back to square #3 from square #11, you would go square #11-8=square #3.

Moving column to column; the formula when the higher square numbers of the board are facing you; which is; the position of the black chess pieces is to move horizontally to the right you would subtract 1 (-1). Example starting on square #64(-1) and that places you on square #63, the direct right square of square #64. To move one square horizontally to the left you would add 1 (+1). Example starting on square #63(+1) and that places you back on square #64. (+1) or (-1) from that particular square number determines your destination of that distinctive chess pieces' particular move at that given point in time.

The Knight Chess piece moves formula:

Formula #6: The Knight chess piece moves are always (+6), (+15), (+17), (+10), (-10), (-17), (-15), (-6).

13

If you want to move a Knight chess piece to the upper left squares (+6) or (+15). If you want to move a Knight chess piece to the upper right squares (+17) or (+10). If you want to move a

Knight chess piece to the lower left squares (-10) or (-17). If you want to move a Knight chess piece to the lower right squares (-15) or (-6). *Notice on some squares you cannot move a Knight because the square numbers would be off the chess board especially considering when the Knight is close to the edges of the chess board.

Knight moves: starting on square #19 to get to the upper left squares, you would go 19+6=square #25;19+15=square #34. To get to the upper right squares you would go 19+17=square #36;19+10=square #29. To get to lower lefts squares you would go 19-10=square #9,19-17=square #2. To get to the lower right squares you would go 19-15= square #4,19-6=square #13.

In general; the formula for knight moves when playing white chess pieces are: (+6), (+15), (+17), (+10) which are; upper square moves and (-6), (-15), (-17), (-10) which are; lower square moves. The formula for knight moves when playing black chess pieces are: (+6), (+15), (+17), (+10) which are; lower square moves and (-6), (-15), (-17), (-10) which are; upper square moves. When playing white chess piece's, you are starting on the lowest number squares. When playing black chess piece's, you are starting on the highest number squares.

Knight moves go forward which is the opposite of the lowest numbers facing you when playing black chess pieces.

14

*Remember forward is (-6), (15), going to the upper left squares and (-17), (-10) is going to the upper right squares.

Knights moves starting on square#46;46-6=square #40, the upper left square. Starting on square #46 again,46-15=square #31 the other upper left square when playing the black chess pieces and all the highest numbers are facing you. Starting on square #46 getting to the upper right squares you would go 46-17=square #29. Starting on square #46 again to get to the other upper right square, you would go 46-10=square#36. To get your black knight to the lower left squares you would (+10) & (+17) e.g. starting on square #46 you would go 46+10=square #56. To get to the other lower left square, you would go 46+17=square #63. To get to the lower right squares you would (+15) & (+6). Starting on square #46, you would go 46+15=square #61 and 46+6=square #52 the other lower right square. *Remember knights' formula for black chess pieces forward moves are: -6, -15, -17, -10 and black knight chess piece backward moves are: +10, +17, +15, +6.

   *Remember the formula for white knight chess piece when going forward are: +6, +15, +17, +10. When white chess pieces are going backwards the formula is: -10, -17, -15, -6.   *

   *Remember all the numbers whether adding or subtracting these numbers stayed the same. Also, remember numbers 9, 8, 7 whether adding or subtracting these numbers also stayed the same. This is easy for playing and recording games.

Assassinatas' Chess 101:

The Assassinatas' start with the black chess pieces going first and the King on his color square not the Queen on her color square. In which, is in differentiation as the old traditional chess system of games in the past. Black chess pieces are on the highest numbers. Which is, rank/row #8; square numbers 57 thru 64. Meaning, blacks king is on square #61 and blacks queen is on square #60. Black pawns are on square numbers: 49,50,51,52,53,54,55,56. Black rooks are on square numbers 57 and 64. Black knights are on square numbers 58 and 63. Black bishops are on square numbers 59 and 62.

White chess pieces are on the lowest square numbers. In which, is rank/row #1, square numbers 1 thru 8. Meaning, white king is on square #4 and white queen is on square #5. White pawns are on square numbers: 9,10,11,12,13,14,15,16. White rooks are on square numbers 1 and 8. White knights are on square numbers 2 and 7. White bishops are on square numbers 3 and 6.

Numeric Notation System:

The Numeric Notation System for recording chess games is slightly different but easier to understand.

Black chess piece positions are:

Black Pawns are on square #'s:56,55,54,53,52,51,50,49;

Black Rooks are on square #'s:64 and 57;

Black Knights are on square #'s:63 and 57;

Black Bishops are on square #'s:62 and 59;

Black Queen is on square # 61 and remember the Assassinatas' Chess Club plays King on his color not Queen on her color like the old tradition. So, that would place Blacks King on square #60 and Black chess pieces go first.

White chess piece positions:

White Pawns are on square #'s:9,10,11,12,13,14,15,16;

White Rooks are on square #'s:1 and 8;

White Knights are on square #'s:2 and 7;

White Bishops are on square #'s:3 and 6;

White Queen is on square #5 and since Assassinatas' Chess Club plays King on his color not Queen on her color the White King is on square #4.

Blacks castling to King side would be Black King over two squares to the right to square #58 and Blacks Rook over two squares to the left to square #59. The notation would look like this 0-0.

Blacks castling to Queen side would be Blacks' King over two squares to the left to square #62 and Blacks Rook moving over three squares to the right to square #61. The notation would look like this 0-0-0.

Whites castling to King side would be Whites King over two squares to the left to square #2 and Whites Rook over two squares to the right to square #3. The notation would look like this 0-0.

Whites castling to Queen side would be Whites King over two squares to the right to square #6 and Whites Rook over three squares to the left to square #5. The notation would look like this 0-0-0.

Castling to King and Queen sides are different the traditional chess because King and Queen chess pieces have been switched. King on his color causing the opposite effect of castling to constitute a 0-0 (Kings castling) and 0-0-0 (Queens castling). Castling is in opposite directions. Castling means to move the King chess piece from his own square two squares to one side and then in the same move; bring the rook from that side to the square immediately past the new position of the King.

18

<u>Symbols:</u>

K=King;

Q=Queen;

R=Rook;

N=Knight;

B=Bishop;

P=Pawn;

The number after the symbol is the actually square # the chess piece moves to and/or lands on, e.g. p36 means pawn to square #36; K46 means King to square #46 etc. If two pieces of the same team can move to the same square the notation would look like this R13 to 12 which means rook on square #13 moves to square #12; or N22 to 28 means Knight on square #22 moves to square #28.

X=capture;

+=check;

0-0=King side castle;

0-0-0=Queen side castle;

1.=blacks first move;

1…=white first move;

(1-0)=black wins;
(1-1)=white wins.

19

e.g.

Black	White
1.p36	p28
2.N46	N19
3.N29	NxN29

4.pxN29 or if two pawns could have taken N29 it would look like p36xN29.

Index…

<u>A</u>

<u>B</u>

<u>C</u>

<u>D</u>

21

22

23

About the Author:

Michael K. Mattox, Sr. was falsely convicted for murder in Topeka, Kansas circa April 2002. This did not deter Mr. Mattox, and thus begun his journey of enhancing his chess game.

In Circa, the year of 2006, Mr. Mattox had gotten very good at the game of chess; this is when another chess playing convict challenged Mr. Mattox to now play and win a game of chess in his head, w/o the board and chess pieces.

Less than a week later, Mr. Mattox got in trouble for trying to get into a personal relationship w/ a female staff member, which is, against the prison handbook rules. Then, Mr. Mattox was sent to solitary confinement, where convicts are locked down in their prison cell for 23 hours or more. This is when Mr. Mattox took the challenge serious.

First, Mr. Mattox begin to develop a formula to memorize every square on the chess board. Second, Mr. Mattox memorize where every chess piece belonged in congruence to those chess squares. When, this was successfully memorized, the third step was playing chess games in his head by his self. Mr. Mattox would then, challenge other chess players in prison to play in their head and Mr. Mattox would also, win those games. After, a while, Mr. Mattox would then break down the chess system in more details and begin to write his findings down; thus this is when "*Cerebral War*" was born.

24